Fountaindale
Public Library

300 W. Briarcliff Road
Bolingbrook, Illinois
60439

BEASTLY RIDDLES

Fishy, Flighty

and Buggy, Too

Beastly

Riddles

JOSEPH LOW

Macmillan Publishing Company
New York

Collier Macmillan Publishers
London

for
Christian

Macmillan Publishing Company,
a division of Macmillan, Inc.
866 Third Avenue, New York, N.Y. 10022
Collier Macmillan Canada, Inc.

Printed in the United States of America
10   9   8   7   6   5   4   3   2   1

Library of Congress Cataloging in Publication Data

Low, Joseph, date.
  Beastly riddles.
  Summary: A collection of riddles pertaining to animals.
  1. Riddles, Juvenile. 2. Animals—Anecdotes,
facetiae, satire, etc. [1. Riddles. 2. Animals—Wit
and humor] I. Title.
PN63715.L59 1983   818′.5402   83-856
ISBN 0-02-761380-1

Which is the most important part of a horse?

The mane part.

The summer visitor asked
how long cows should be milked.

"Same as short ones,"
said the farmer.

Why are chickens not welcome at the dinner table?

Because they use such fowl language.

What kind of cat should you never
play cards with?

A cheetah.

Which animals brought
the largest luggage aboard Noah's ark?

The elephants had
the biggest trunks.

Why would anyone want to look like a crow?

Be caws.

Why don't mosquitoes
annoy a sleeping man?

Because it's only when he wakes up that he is annoyed.

Where, out of water, can you
find some types of fish?

There's a perch in
every birdcage,

skates on frozen ponds, and

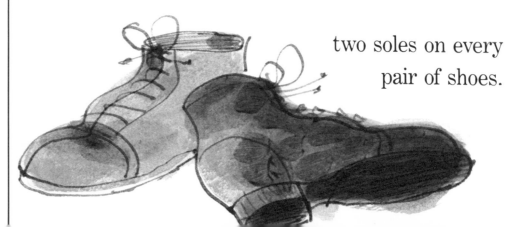

two soles on every
pair of shoes.

Why is a pig in the parlor
like a house on fire?

The sooner it is put out, the better.

What would you say if your goat swallowed my rabbit?

Your hare
is in my butter.

Why does the camel get into so many fights?

He always has his back up
about something.

If you call an elephant's trunk his leg,
how many legs will he have?

Four.

A horse like a bird?
How can that be?

Have you never seen a horsefly?

How does the rooster
keep his feathers
so nicely groomed?

He carries his comb
wherever he goes.

What is the key to a proper Thanksgiving dinner?

A turkey.

Why is a watchdog longer at night than during the day?

Because he is let out at night and taken in during the day.

My Uncle August challenged a lion on Friday. So how do I know Saturday was the first day of September?

Because Friday was the last of August.

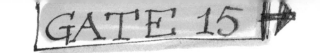

Why is a goldfish
like an experienced traveler?

He has been around the globe so many times.

What do the people in Zanzibar
call their small cats?

Kittens.

Why does a wasp seldom lose an argument?

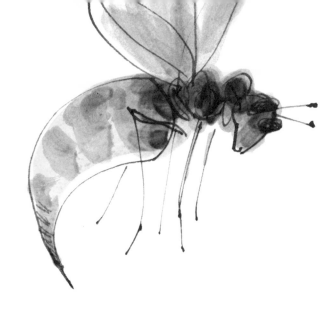

She has such a convincing point
at the end.

How can I keep my brother's horse
from using our bathtub?

Pull the plug out.

Why should a chicken never put her secret money in a bank operated by a Swiss rabbit?

Because she may never
see hide nor hare
of it again.